Grant Area District Library

122 Elder Ave
Grant, MI 49327

JOB BASICS™
GETTING THE JOB YOU NEED

GETTING A JOB IN
ACCOUNTING

AMY BEATTIE

Published in 2017 by The Rosen Publishing Group, Inc.
29 East 21st Street, New York, NY 10010

First Edition

Library of Congress Cataloging-in-Publication Data

Names: Beattie, Amy.
Title: Getting a job in accounting / Amy Beattie.
Description: New York : Rosen Publishing, 2017. | Series: Job basics | Includes index.
Identifiers: ISBN 9781477785607 (library bound)
Subjects: LCSH: Accounting--Vocational guidance--Juvenile literature. | Accounting--Juvenile literature.
Classification: LCC HF5657.B43 2017 | DDC 657'.023'73--dc23

Manufactured in China

CONTENTS

INTRODUCTION

At first glance, accounting might appear to be a tedious industry that consists of crunching numbers in spreadsheets all day long. But in fact, accounting encompasses many different roles related to corporate and personal finance. It can be an exciting field for anyone who is interested in business, good at math, skilled with computers, and able to communicate well with others.

Accountants are important members of just about every company. They are responsible for billing and accounts, ensuring that businesses are financially stable and profitable. Although some accountants focus exclusively on bookkeeping and recording transactions, many other accountants coordinate with clients and coworkers constantly in order to ensure that they are meeting their projections and financial goals.

An accountant might be in charge of all aspects of accounting at a small, locally owned business, or she might be a member of an accounting team with several different departments in a large corporation. Accountants who specialize in certain areas might focus on costs, budgets, management, or financial outlooks.

Accountants also help individuals and businesses file their tax returns each year. Related to this field is auditing, an investigation that checks whether taxes have been filed properly and that all other finances are handled legally. Forensic accounting is another subfield that deals with investigating fraud or other financial wrongdoing. For example, a forensic accountant might be hired by a prosecutor to examine someone's finances and then testify in a criminal case.

Students who are interested in accounting should focus on doing well in their high school math courses, though other classes will also be beneficial both in college and the workplace. A familiarity with spreadsheets and other computer programs will be a plus going forward, whether you work toward your accounting certificate, an associate's degree, or a bachelor's degree.

Some accountant positions require certain degrees and certification exams, but there is still flexibility. You can start out in a lower-level position and eventually work your way up. Some employers might pay (in part or in full) for an employee to go back to school and advance his career. Another option is to earn your bachelor's degree and pass the exam to become a certified public accountant (CPA) before getting a job.

Either way, as with most jobs, candidates for accounting positions will need to prepare a résumé and cover letter. They'll need to find out about job openings through job websites, word of mouth, and networking. Finally, they will interview for positions until finally being offered a job that is the right fit, both for the applicant and the employer.

Accountants nowadays do much of their work through computer programs, but calculators and adding machines remain useful and widespread today.

Putting in all this work can be stressful, but the effort is worth it once you land your first accounting job and begin progressing in your career. Accounting is a growing field, so there will always be opportunities for hardworking, talented young job candidates. According to the Bureau of Labor Statistics, there will be an 11 percent increase in available accounting jobs over the next few years. Before you know it, you could have an entry-level job in accounting and be working your way toward becoming a CPA.

CHAPTER ONE

Exploring the Accounting Field

Although accounting might seem like a straightforward field, there are many different jobs that fall under its umbrella, such as auditor, bookkeeper, payroll accountant, cost accountant, and tax accountant. Certified public accountants (CPAs) wear many hats and often do different tasks for different clients. Let's take a look at the major functions of accounting and why they are done.

Major Functions of Accounting

Have you ever found money in your pocket and forgotten where it came from? Perhaps you've checked your bank account balance online or at an ATM and saw less than you expected. Where did all of the money go? Losing track of a few dollars here and there is not a big deal for one person, but it can be a disaster for a business. If a corporation does not keep careful track of all its finances, it may be unable to pay its employees or may even go bankrupt. Accountants and accounting firms are essential because they track how much money a particular business, individual, or institution takes in daily, weekly, monthly, quarterly, and annually.

Recording payments or income incorrectly or in the wrong places can significantly affect the financial statements for a business. In the United States, every registered business—whether a sole proprietor or a huge corporation like Apple, Inc.—must provide proper records for the Internal Revenue Service (IRS), the federal government agency that collects tax revenue and establishes taxation laws. Proper financial recordkeeping helps determine how much a business pays in taxes each year.

It is illegal for a company to purposely withhold or provide incorrect financial statements to the IRS. Otherwise, it leaves itself open to sanctions, such as fines and even possible jail time for the person or people responsible. That's why it's so important to record each and every transaction that occurs in a business.

Accountants—especially CPAs—guide the financial direction of businesses by also providing predictions about future business growth, sometimes called projections. In larger firms and big companies with many branches, they collect and analyze financial data from different departments. They need to assess the costs of various business processes, insurance, stock performance, human resources and payroll, materials and supplies, taxes, fees, liabilities, and much more. They may do periodical and detailed investigations of all of a company's finances, called audits.

Where Accountants Work

A large company may have different teams of accountants in different departments. For example, a chain of department stores may have a team of accountants that oversee their warehouse and logistics operations, and another that carefully watches their retail profits. Higher up, a group led by the chief financial officer (CFO) leads all of these teams. These are considered in-house or corporate accountants.

Meanwhile, public accountants work at accounting firms that hire themselves out to clients. These may be other companies that require their services. In this manner, they act

Keeping track of your own purchases and ATM withdrawals is a simplified version of what accountants do.

much like a separate accounting department for that firm. Even large corporations may retain the service of a separate but integrated accounting firm. The main large accounting firms in the United States and Canada are known as the Big Four: KPMG, Ernst & Young, Deloitte Touch Tohmatsu, and PricewaterhouseCoopers (PwC).

The IRS is the government agency responsible for processing all individuals' and businesses' tax returns, which are often prepared by accountants.

TRANSACTIONS AND DOUBLE-ENTRY ACCOUNTING

One way to explore whether you may have a passion for or aptitude in accounting is to get a sense of one of the most basic tasks that defines this job. A transaction is an event that changes the balance of at least two accounts. The accounting system that is used by accounting professionals is called double-entry accounting.

Double-entry accounting states that for every one transaction that occurs, there will be at least two accounts affected. One account will be debited, or have money subtracted. This is usually marked on the left side of an account when a purchase has been made. The other account will be credited, or have money added. This will be marked on the right side of the account to show that a payment has been received. Together, these actions complete one transaction.

In order to record business transactions, you need to first examine the transaction and decide which accounts will be affected. Then you have to decide which account will be debited and which account will be credited. After that you will document the transaction in a journal.

A journal, which is also known as a book of original entry, is the first place that a transaction is entered in accounting records. Even when you're using a computerized accounting program, items are still recorded in journals, even if they are not manually entered by hand but rather into the software itself.

The best way to learn how to record business transactions is to practice. A great exercise is to keep a list of your personal expenses for one week. During this week, list everything you've earned next to the date you receive your money. On the next page, list everything you've spent next to the day you make the purchase. This is the very basic format of how companies, both large and small, record transactions, a practice otherwise known as bookkeeping.

Accountants often use stamps to mark which expenses have been paid.
Sometimes, they even have stamps for each date. Modern accounting
methods often track payments and other transactions digitally.

Other accounting firms focus solely on tax preparation. These may include small businesses made up of only one accountant, or two to three of them, plus supporting staff. Small businesses and individuals hire companies like this to help them do their taxes and maximize their tax refunds and minimize their tax liabilities (what they have to pay). The tax preparation industry also includes retail tax preparation chains with hundreds of branches, including well-known firms like H&R Block, Jackson Hewitt, Liberty Tax, and others.

Governments (at the federal, state, and local levels) and nonprofit organizations also need to employ accountants to manage their finances.

Bookkeeping vs. Accounting

Bookkeeping is a major component of accounting, but it can also be considered a slightly different job and career than accounting proper, though the two are very much related, and many of their tasks overlap.

The job of bookkeepers is a crucial one and can involve, but is not limited to, the following: recording basic, daily transactions, such as debits and credits; generating invoices (records of goods or services provided, with an amount due for them); and cutting checks and payments to vendors, employees (called payroll), and others owed money by a company. Until they grow large enough, many business owners even handle bookkeeping on their own, with the use of retail accounting software such as Quickbooks.

Many bookkeepers, especially in small businesses, begin in entry-level jobs, such as data entry, or as assistants to bookkeepers or accountants. They usually learn on the job and gain promotions over time due to seniority (how long they have been around) and merit.

While those with more experience can attain their own professional certifications, bookkeepers are often considered a step beneath accountants in the hierarchy of bigger businesses and organizations, even if they work alongside each other. As Laurie Reeves writes for Demand Media, bookkeepers are "considered by accountants and CPAs as just technicians or clerks." Still, they perform invaluable tasks and can be considered the troops on the ground, if accountants are midlevel superiors.

The minimum education required of bookkeepers is a high school diploma, or a General Educational Development (GED) degree. Many business and trade schools provide training in bookkeeping, as do two-year community colleges, which can help entry-level bookkeepers get better jobs. Certificates from business schools and associate's degrees will translate into better pay and career opportunities, even early on.

TYPES OF ACCOUNTING

Within the field of accounting, there are several different paths available. For example, tax accounting focuses on preparing tax returns and adhering to tax codes. Budgetary accounting deals with managing a company's budget, while cost accounting assesses all the costs associated with a business, such as materials, labor, and overhead.

Auditors are accountants who review businesses' financial records to make sure that their financial practices are fair. Some large companies might have their own auditing department, though most businesses hire an independent auditing firm. Companies can also be subject to an external audit from the government. Usually this would be the IRS checking to make sure that a company has paid all its taxes.

Another type of accounting that deals with investigative work is forensic accounting. Forensic accountants examine financial documents to uncover evidence of illegal activity, such as money laundering or embezzlement. They may be hired by law enforcement, lawyers, or insurance agents, and they may need to testify in court about the financial crimes they discover.

Beyond Bookkeeping: What Accountants Do

Accountants usually do work beyond bookkeeping and are drawn from college graduates who major in accounting, business, or similar degree programs. Even general business majors (students who received a bachelor's in business administration) can become accountants. In large organizations or offices, because of their place on a higher rung of the ladder, accountants usually oversee clerks and other subordinates who do much of the data entry and paperwork. They make up the financial backbone of most businesses. In some

Tax preparation chains, such as Liberty Tax, help customers file their taxes with the IRS. These businesses often experience their busiest season just before the annual April 15 deadline for taxpayers to file.

cases, the work done by an entry-level accountant or an accounting clerk might be the same as a bookkeeper, but the former are usually on a longer and more professional career track.

Accountants coordinate and manage many of the big-picture financial functions of business, beyond simply recording trans-actions, profit and loss, and other bookkeeping duties. They often review these tasks done by lower-level employees, and they answer to accounting managers.

Certified Public Accountants (CPAs)

At the top of the accounting profession are those who have attained the title of certified public accountant (CPA). To become certified, candidates must pass the Uniform Certified Public Accountant Examination. All fifty states of the United

States recognize this exam as the official certification for the accounting profession.

The American Institute of Certified Public Accountants (AICPA) is the official body and professional organization that administers the test and generally oversees the rules governing the accounting profession. This includes maintaining ethical and legal standards for individual accountants and accounting firms. The AICPA also establishes the rules by which companies, nonprofit organizations, and governments and government agencies at all levels must keep their books in case they get audited.

Before they can even pass the examination, accountants must attain a certain amount of experience, which differs among the states. Once they pass the exam, their status as CPAs gives both potential employers and clients information about their skills and professional standing.

Most independent accounting firms are run by CPAs, and clients, such as those who seek accountants for tax preparations, will almost always choose CPAs before non-certified accountants. Even people in the highest managerial positions of finance, such as controller, and top-level executive posts, such as chief financial officer (CFO), are usually if not always CPAs.

Do You Have What It Takes?

Before you embark on this career track, ask yourself if you have what it takes and if it suits your likes and sensibilities.

Accounting can be a tough job, and depending on the position, it can require long and sometimes tedious and stressful hours crunching numbers. You need to be comfortable with and actually enjoy not only basic mathematics but also statistics and other complex calculations and financial projections. Accountants should be masters at multitasking, detail-oriented, and comfortable working in generally conservative and buttoned-up office environments. They also need to be tech-savvy and willing to learn new accounting and office software, with frequent changes and upgrades. In addition, they need to be able to get along with coworkers and clients, and, perhaps most important, perform their jobs accurately and ethically.

If you know you have what it takes, let's get started and explore the schooling and training necessary to get a job in accounting.

CHAPTER TWO

An Education in Accounting

Accounting is a highly specialized field that demands intensive training and study. How far you go up the career ladder depends entirely on you. Students who have a knack for numbers and an analytical mind can get started early by building their skills and talents. They can begin paving the way as early as high school.

A Visit to Your High School Guidance Counselor

At most every school, helpful staff members are on hand to help students with one of the most important decisions they will ever make: what to do after high school. Besides counseling teens on how to go about applying to educational institutions after they graduate, high school guidance counselors also take a hands-on, big-picture approach to helping them.

Guidance counselors make it a point to learn the strengths and weaknesses of the students that visit them. They can help determine what classes to take (and in what order) to best achieve an individual student's goals. This is true for all students, including aspiring accountants.

Counselors might encourage them to participate in extra-curricular activities that will help them, such as joining math team competitions and leagues. Some schools even have accounting clubs, while other extracurricular groups such as computer clubs can help students develop some of the skills that are useful for future accountants.

What Classes to Take

A guidance counselor will encourage you to take classes in a few subject areas that will sharpen your aptitude with numbers and analytical and problem-solving abilities. Advanced Placement (AP) classes and other higher-level mathematics courses are encouraged. Some of the ones offered by many schools are algebra I and II, advanced algebra, calculus, discrete mathematics, computer math, probability and statistics, and trigonometry. Even classes that focus on personal budgeting and finance, such as home economics, can be useful. Even if the specific subject matter in such classes seems like it has little to do with hands-on bookkeeping, it can help math students keep their skills sharp.

Counselors will underscore that you should also take courses that will make you well-rounded as a student and as an accountant. These include classes in English and writing, communications, and business administration. Taking a class in office software and/or business applications, including Microsoft Office, is especially important. Spreadsheet programs like Excel provide a crucial foundation for learning more complicated and specialized accounting software later on.

College in High School: Aim Higher

If your school offers them—and many do—and you show you have what it takes, you should try to sign up for college credits in accounting and related subjects while you are still in high school. This will give you a head's up on the things you will later need to master. Even better, you will also save money by being able to transfer credits once you do graduate.

College-level accounting, math, and business classes may take place on-site at your own school. You may also take credits offered on a college campus, either in classes offered exclusively to visiting high schoolers or by actually sitting in on introductory courses with college students.

Earning college credit can be an exciting opportunity to immerse yourself in the subject and make connections with faculty and teaching assistants,

An invaluable resource to students, guidance counselors can help you plan your next steps after high school as you progress toward your goal of working in accounting.

These high school students in Colorado are participating in the Deloitte Virtual Team Challenge, which simulates real-life business situations and scenarios often handled by accountants.

especially if you plan on attending the school full-time later. Regardless of where you go, make sure the commute to a separate campus works for your schedule and does not interfere with other potential classes or your other responsibilities, like volunteering, family obligations, or an after-school job.

Financial Aid: What to Know

As your high school career progresses, you will spend more and more time preparing for the ultimate goal: graduation and furthering your education after high school. This includes the sometimes intimidating and tedious process of arranging to take and practicing for standardized college admissions tests, including the Scholastic Aptitude Test (SAT) and earlier scholarship competitions and achievement tests.

（GETTING A JOB IN **ACCOUNTING**）

Guidance counselors, teachers, parents, and trusted adults can all help you negotiate the processes of applying for financial aid, including student scholarships, awards, grants, and loans. It can seem intimidating and stressful at first, but most of the work involved in filling out these forms is straightforward.

A good test run might be to try to fill out some forms on your own, with whatever information you can come up with—after all, as an accountant, you will be doing quite a bit of paperwork, both on hard copy and, more often, via computer. With any applications, even if you try them out to get accustomed to the process, always have someone with financial aid experience check your work because it's easy to miss an important detail. You can then fill them out again if needed.

It is crucial that you fill out all forms completely and accurately, or you may needlessly miss out on opportunities you could have easily exploited. Make sure to familiarize yourself with all the deadlines you will need to meet. Set up a calendar on your phone or computer, and back it up with a written one hanging at your desk or in your room. Also, make sure to go online to verify that deadlines and application procedures have not somehow changed.

Knowing Your Options

Federal, state, and even local money is available to many students who qualify. You can consult with your guidance counselor on what exactly might work best for you. Besides the usual application for federal aid, you may be able to investigate scholarships provided by schools themselves.

There are also many organizations that may provide merit-based scholarships to worthy students. These can include local chambers of commerce; local, regional and national business associations, including the American Institute of CPAs; religious groups and faith-based organizations of all stripes; alumni groups associated with your school of choice or even your high school; groups that help women and members of ethnic minorities increase their representation in the accounting workforce; and various charitable foundations.

Staff at college admissions offices and financial aid officers can help prospective students find ways to make their higher education experience more affordable.

Active U.S. military personnel and veterans can also take advantage of various government and private programs that help them jump-start accounting careers.

Accounting Classes: Beyond High School

You now have your high school diploma. Congratulations! Depending on your job goals in accounting, you are on your way to one of several types of institutions: a business or technical school, a two-year community college, or a four-year institution like a college or university. There are different financial aid packages for each, and in addition to your own high school staff helping you out, any reputable schools will offer personal assistance to help you figure out your financial aid options.

Accounting Certificates

If you want to land an entry-level accounting job sooner rather than later, you can opt to take a very focused accounting program that yields a certificate. Programs are offered by both business and trade schools, also called vocational schools, as well as colleges and universities.

Most programs cover about six to eight courses that give someone a basic foundation in bookkeeping and/or accounting, depending the specific focus of the program. But most or all of the classes will deal with the core skills needed to get a job right away, including training in the necessary basic software (such as Peachtree, Excel, and QuickBooks); mathematics

APPLYING FOR AID USING FAFSA

The one major application that nearly everyone fills out is the Free Application for Federal Student Aid (FAFSA). More often than not, teens nowadays submit this application online. It can also be done by phone or by filling out a hard copy application on paper, usually available at your high school guidance or college placement office.

The different kinds of aid available fall into three main categories:

Grants: A grant is money given out by the government to help students pay for school, which does not need to be paid back. Historically, the most common federal education grant has been Pell Grants. These are need-based, meaning they are given to students who demonstrate academic excellence and promise but who may not have enough money (either personally or from their family) to fully pay for college themselves. If you enter an accounting program partly paid for with grants and don't complete it, you may be liable to return part or all of the money, depending on the arrangement.

Loans: Low interest student loans are available through the federal government. These can take the form of direct student loans provided through the Federal Direct Student Loan Program, which includes well-known ones such as the Stafford Loan and the Federal Perkins Loan. These are paid out and owed back to the U.S. government directly, hence their name. Others are obtained from private lenders with federal help.

Work-study: Work-study programs let students work off part of their tuition or other fees as school employees. Useful experiences for accounting students on work study may be helping out with bookkeeping in student administration, including the bursar's office, or anywhere else where they can sharpen their math, computer, or communication skills..

for business and finance; financial, managerial, and cost accounting; and financial management.

You can usually find programs that work with your schedule, especially if you are already working full-time while getting your certificate after hours. There are even many online options to learn as well. The drawbacks to such programs are that they are not as in-depth as more intensive programs, and they do limit the holder to lower-level and entry-level work.

Though applying for aid through FAFSA might seem intimidating, it's also vital in order to receive federal grants and loans.

Associate's and Bachelor's Degrees

A step up from a certificate, a two-year or associate's degree can be the stepping stone to immediate work as a clerk, bookkeeper, or accounting assistant. It can also be a path to a four-year degree if you can transfer your credits. The core classes in accounting and bookkeeping are supplemented with other liberal arts requirements to gain your degree, including English, communication, public speaking courses, and more. The later coursework in accounting and book-keeping is often at a higher level than most of the courses in a certificate program.

Obtaining a four-year degree is an even better bet for those who want to get better jobs in accounting. A bachelor's degree in business administration or related disciplines can get you a job in accounting. But a bachelor of arts in business administration in accounting, or a bachelor of science in accounting (BS/ACC), is the most likely road to starting an accounting career. These provide you with the most advanced training of the three listed thus far, including more intensive coursework that situates accounting within the larger fields of finance and business generally.

Certified Public Accountants

The pinnacle, or height, of one's education and training in accounting is to become a certified public accountant (CPA). This requires further schooling on top of a bachelor's degree. Some opt to go to graduate school to obtain a master's in accounting, but students can also take the necessary additional courses without enrolling in a degree program.

Many states require at least 150 semester hours of further training beyond a bachelor's before they allow someone to sit for the Uniform CPA Examination, and also at least one year of work experience, working under the supervision of an actual CPA. The official body that administers the test is the National Association of State Boards of Accountancy (NASBA), which also helps set individual states' requirements for test-takers. One of these may even be getting a probationary license in accounting before being able to take the test.

It is one of the tougher professional accreditation exams out there, akin to the bar exam for attorneys. Passing it requires intense dedication and a tremendous amount of

Upper-level positions at accounting firms are almost exclusively held by people who have passed the Uniform CPA Examination.

studying and practice. It covers attestation and auditing, financial accounting and reporting, financial regulation, and business environments and concepts. In many states, those who pass the exam must also pass a professional conduct and/or ethics test, too.

While a B.A. or B.S. can help you land jobs in corporate and management accounting, becoming a CPA opens up possibilities of advancement, including management- and executive-track opportunities in many companies and types of accounting. CPAs command the most respect and best-paying positions in their field. Becoming a CPA is also necessary to advance to the most interesting and important jobs that accountants can hold in other related fields, such as law enforcement, government, public accounting, auditing/assurance, and compliance.

CHAPTER THREE

Building a Résumé and the Job Search

Now that you've obtained your desired degree and/or certification, it's time to look for a job. The first thing to do is to create a professional résumé. This is a one-page summary of all of your educational and work experience, which employers will read to determine whether you have the necessary skills and experience to do the job for which they're hiring.

Beyond your résumé, you'll also often need to write a cover letter that outlines why you are a good candidate for the position. Many employers ask for references from people who can speak to your abilities. This might be a former boss or teacher.

A successful job search combines several strategies so that you're aware of all the possible opportunities in your area. Searching online job sites is a great tool to find a job, but you should also probably try to meet people in the accounting field or visit nearby employment agencies.

Once you see which companies are hiring, you'll want to research them and find out if they'd be a good place to work. For example, working at a small company might allow you to learn more about different types of accounting, but a more specific role at a big company might offer more opportunity

Employers use résumés to determine quickly whether an applicant has the skills and experience needed to do a particular job. An attractive résumé will lead employers to call you in for job interviews.

for growth in the future. Knowing these kinds of things can help you decide what kind of job environment you'd prefer working in.

It can be a lot of work, but it definitely pays off when you land the right job for you. Looking for a job requires the same determination and care that you need to pursue any other goal, such as applying to college, making the varsity team, or practicing a difficult piece of music.

Designing Your Résumé

Even though a résumé is required in order to be hired for just about any job, many job seekers don't put enough effort into designing the perfect résumé. The résumé is usually the first item that an employer looks at when assessing candidates for a job. Even before someone starts to read a résumé to see whether the candidate is qualified, he or she will notice the overall presentation of the résumé. To get an idea of how résumés should be structured, search online for résumé examples and templates.

If you obtained your degree in accounting or have earned your certification, those achievements demonstrate your abilities in the field. But on-the-job experience from part-time work or internships in accounting can be equally advantageous. Employers value both education and experience, though depending on their needs, they might prefer one over the other.

Résumés can also include experience that, at first glance, might not seem relevant to obtaining a job in accounting. First and foremost, especially for entry-level positions, hiring managers are looking for a person who is responsible, reliable, and willing and able to learn. Just about any part-time job or volunteer experience can apply to that, whether you babysat for the same family for several years or you planned a big fundraiser at your school.

Your résumé should be easy to read, but not boring—you want to stand out from the competition. A résumé should follow a standard format throughout. For example, you might want to put all of your job titles in italic font and all of the company names in bold so that they stand out when some-one first glances at it. All of the margins and bullet points need to line up. Experiment with different fonts and text size

Government labor offices, such as this New York State Department of Labor branch, can help job seekers find openings in their field.

RECOMMENDATIONS AND REFERENCES

Teens should keep contact information for trusted adults who will recommend them for work. Employers will rely on these people to make sure that job applicants are trustworthy and reliable. These contacts can include:

- Former employers, including anyone you have worked for, including retail, restaurant, or other service work. Naturally, recommendations from qualified accountants will perhaps have the greatest impact on your chances.
- Teachers, instructors, or professors, especially for course work in math, accounting, or computers.
- Leaders or members of community groups, nonprofits, churches, and other organizations in which you may have participated or assumed a leadership role.

If a hiring manager asks for references, that usually means he or she will call or email the people on your list to ask them about you. If the hiring managers asks for recommendations, that usually refers to letters that your supervisor or teacher has written about you ahead of time for just this purpose.

to make sure that it looks professional and clean and fits on one page.

Most important of all is to proofread. A misspelling on your résumé tells a hiring manager that you don't care about details. Best of all, ask a friend, parent, or teacher to look over your résumé before you submit it to any employers. Someone with a fresh pair of eyes will probably catch a couple of mistakes that you missed because you've read the same material so many times.

Writing a Cover Letter

Even though a résumé sums up all of your qualifications in one page, many job postings will require you to submit a cover letter as well. In a few paragraphs, you should explain why you're interested in the position and what makes you a good candidate for it. Try not to use the same words from your résumé because whoever is reading your cover letter will be looking at your résumé, too, and you don't want to seem boring or repetitive.

It's a good idea to draft out a sample cover letter that you could use for many different job applications. However, you should later edit it to customize it for the skills and requirements given in a particular job listing. Just as with your résumé, proofreading your cover letter for typos and other mistakes is vital. Before submitting any cover letter, make sure you didn't accidentally put the wrong position or company in the subject or first line!

Employment Websites

Armed with a résumé and cover letter template, you're ready to start applying for positions. Job websites can be a great place to find a variety of open positions in your area. The largest online job websites are aggregator sites. Along with direct employer postings, they collect job listings from other websites and search engines from all across the Internet. Some of the more popular job sites include Indeed, Monster, CareerBuilder, Simply Hired, Snagajob, Dice, JobBankUSA, and EmploymentGuide.

The key to success with these sites is to know what parameters to enter in order to narrow your search. If you simply search for "accounting," the site will pull all the job listings that mention the word "accounting." These may include positions at all levels, including upper-level management, or jobs that are in entirely different fields but happen to mention accounting in the job description.

One way to help narrow your searches is to find out what job titles are used for the types of positions in which you're interested and for which you're qualified. Entry-level positions often have the word "assistant" in their job titles, so adding that to a search might help narrow the results to positions that you'll be qualified for. Or the website may allow you to limit your search to jobs that are considered entry level.

Timing is also very important when looking for jobs on job aggregator sites. Pay attention to the date on which the jobs were listed. Sometimes companies leave their job listings up on the Internet for months. A job that was posted two months earlier may have already been filled. However, that doesn't necessarily mean that you shouldn't put in an application. It's also possible that the hiring manager hasn't found the right person yet and is still interviewing for the position.

Once you've found some positions to apply for, it's time to submit your application. Be sure to carefully follow all of the directions on how to apply. Some companies might ask you to send an email to a particular address. You might be told to attach your résumé as a certain file type, or you may have to put the job title in the email subject line. Other companies might require you to fill out an online application of their own design. If you don't follow all the instructions, your

Employment sites like Monster are a good way to find lots of jobs to apply for, but you should also experiment with and utilize other strategies to find accounting positions.

application will probably be dismissed, even if you're a good candidate for the position.

Trade and Industry Journals

Trade and industry journals, both online and print editions, are also a potential source for job seekers. Online editions available to the public occasionally host their own job boards. Publications without free online access, or with subscriptions restricted to actual industry employees, may sometimes be found at the library. They are also good sources for discovering how an industry works, brushing up on the latest trends, and sparking more job-hunting ideas. Some great accounting journals are:

- *Journal of Accountancy*
- *Accounting Today*
- *CPA Journal*
- *Journal of Accounting Research*
- *Journal of Forensic and Investigative Accounting*
- *International Journal of Accounting*
- *CPA Trendlines*

Networking

Connecting with people you know from different areas of life can be a great way to find a new job. Maybe your friends and family don't work in accounting, but they know someone who does, and that person might be willing to help you in your job search. Other people who might be able to help include members of your religious community, sports team, or community service group.

At job fairs or other networking events, and at job interviews, it's important to exchange contact information with the people you meet. Look into making business cards with your own information on them.

Alumni from your college or high school are often eager to give advice to new graduates. Often, they received help from older alumni when they were first starting their career, so they like to return the favor. In the future, you may also want to help younger students. You can find contacts through your school, and then write to these alumni asking them if they'd be willing to meet you and tell you about their experiences in the accounting field.

Thus, although "networking" can seem overwhelming, all it really means is making the most of the connections you already have, and then continuing to meet more people who can advise you. Start by putting the word out among your friends and family members that you are seeking employment in accounting. Most often, the people in your network will jump at the chance to help you.

Email contacts individually every once in a while, and remain friendly with former bosses, instructors, and others with industry connections. People who network frequently hear about jobs even before they are advertised to the general public. Employers receive dozens or even hundreds of résumés for every position. Candidates known to them, or recommended to them by someone they trust, will have a better chance than strangers with otherwise similar backgrounds and experience.

Go Get It!

A great accounting job is not going to land in your lap—you have to put in the work to find it. Another idea is to visit the businesses in your local area. This gives you a chance to personally get to know more successful people where you live. Always dress professionally when visiting potential employers.

Let them know you are seeking employment, and ask if there is anything available in the finance department. Someone will usually instruct you to leave a copy of your physical résumé that can be kept on file for when positions become available.

The only way to find a job is to be proactive. A combination of online job searches, networking, and other research will help you land interviews.

CHAPTER FOUR

Interviewing for an Accounting Job

With determination and hard work, you will eventually be contacted to schedule a job interview. Your résumé and cover letter got you in the door, but now you need to impress the hiring manager in person or, occasionally, over the phone. A phone interview is sometimes the first stage in the hiring process, and then the most preferred candidates will be asked to come in for a face-to-face interview. Either way, preparing for an interview is like studying for a test in school: it drastically increases your chances of success.

Preparing for an Interview

It's natural to be nervous before an interview, especially if you haven't been on many in the past. Practicing and researching ahead of time goes a long way toward reducing this tension. It's a good idea to prepare answers for some typical interview questions, such as: "Why are you interested in this position?" "What are your goals for the future?" "Tell me about a time when you showed initiative and leadership in the workplace."

Despite the often technical nature, many jobs in accounting require good people skills to deal with clients. Make sure to keep this in mind when interviewing. Your friendliness reflects on how you willl deal with coworkers and clients.

Then, ask a friend or family member to conduct a mock interview with you. This will enhance your public speaking skills and help you sound confident and knowledgeable in the real interview. Although you don't want to sound too rehearsed, the more you practice giving answers to these types of questions, the more relaxed you'll be when a stranger is asking them.

You should also research the company and the duties and responsibilities of the position you are interviewing for. Be prepared with at least three questions for your interviewers to further engage conversation and to show that you've done your research.

Make it a habit to check your email at least once a day in case you receive responses from potential employers. If your voicemail is not professional, be sure to redo your voicemail greeting, including your full name and a pleasant invite for the caller to leave a detailed message on your voicemail. Review all of the instructions and guidelines in all communication with the employer and respond to them in a timely fashion. If possible, write back or return calls the same day or within twenty-four hours. Managers might receive dozens or even hundreds of responses for particular positions. Unless someone shows immediate interest after being contacted, employers will quickly move on to the next candidate.

Final Preparations

Be sure to provide the interviewer with your phone number, preferably a mobile number if possible, so that he or she can reach you in case the interview date or time changes. Appointments are sometimes cancelled at the last minute, and you want to be sure he or she is able to inform you if that is the case. Similarly, ask the interviewer for his or her contact number in case you get lost or delayed and need to ask for directions.

It's best to map out your commute to and from the interview or worksite as soon as you confirm the meeting time and place. You should always arrive about fifteen minutes early for an interview. This shows your punctuality and makes a good first impression. When traveling, include a cushion for travel delays. For example, if the travel time from your house to an interview site is one hour, give yourself an extra half hour for possible delays. If there is any confusion, ask the contact person for exact details, including time and address. Never assume anything, and do not be embarrassed to ask; it is better to find out for sure than to guess and end up in the wrong place.

The Interview

Meeting a prospective employer can be nerve-racking. Smile, offer a firm handshake, and be confident and relaxed. Showing

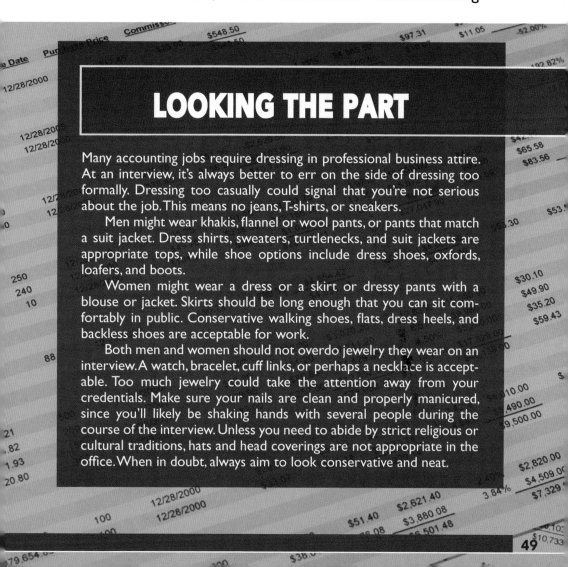

LOOKING THE PART

Many accounting jobs require dressing in professional business attire. At an interview, it's always better to err on the side of dressing too formally. Dressing too casually could signal that you're not serious about the job. This means no jeans, T-shirts, or sneakers.

Men might wear khakis, flannel or wool pants, or pants that match a suit jacket. Dress shirts, sweaters, turtlenecks, and suit jackets are appropriate tops, while shoe options include dress shoes, oxfords, loafers, and boots.

Women might wear a dress or a skirt or dressy pants with a blouse or jacket. Skirts should be long enough that you can sit comfortably in public. Conservative walking shoes, flats, dress heels, and backless shoes are acceptable for work.

Both men and women should not overdo jewelry they wear on an interview. A watch, bracelet, cuff links, or perhaps a necklace is acceptable. Too much jewelry could take the attention away from your credentials. Make sure your nails are clean and properly manicured, since you'll likely be shaking hands with several people during the course of the interview. Unless you need to abide by strict religious or cultural traditions, hats and head coverings are not appropriate in the office. When in doubt, always aim to look conservative and neat.

Most offices where accountants work tend to be formal work environments. Even if a company may generally be thought of as casual when it comes to its dress code, your best bet is to wear a suit to job interviews.

up early and introducing yourself to the receptionist is a great start. You'll need to give the receptionist your name and explain whom you're meeting and why.

When interviewing, answer questions in detail, knowledgeably, and in complete sentences. Try not to ramble on, offer unnecessary details, or exhibit nervous behavior. Avoid "pause words" and "conversation filler"—words such as "um," "uh," and "like"— that demonstrate anxiety and uncertainty. Other nervous activity includes excessive finger tapping, leg shaking, biting on one's fingernails, or playing with pens or pencils, including doodling on paper.

Applicants should give the interviewer their full attention, listen carefully to everything that is said, and answer questions fully. Also, if you're not quite sure how to answer a question right away, don't panic! It's okay to take a moment or two to think about

GETTING A JOB IN **ACCOUNTING**

what to say, rather than just spitting out the first thing that comes to mind.

Be honest about work experience, skills, and training. Instead of focusing on what you don't know, you want to emphasize that you are sharp and a fast learner. The worst thing you could do is lie about knowing how to work a specific program. You may be asked to perform a task on the spot or immediately upon hire.

Job applicants should always strive to be engaging, friendly, and knowledgeable during an interview.

Remember: no one expects applicants at the entry level to be experts in industry lingo, practices, or programs. It is more important for interviewees to be presentable, energetic, enthusiastic, and professional. Experienced professionals will often see right through false claims. If the candidate is not right for the job, both parties will be better off if the match does not work out.

Following Up After an Interview

Common professional courtesy demands that interviewees send a letter of thanks to anyone they met during the interview process (excluding a receptionist). Although taking the time to send a thank-you letter in the mail can be a nice touch, some hiring managers will make their decision so quickly that a letter might not reach them in time. Others may not look at their physical mail as often as their email, so emailing may be the best option. Be sure to ask all of the people you meet for their contact information or business card if you don't already have it.

In the follow-up letter, you should thank everyone for his or her time, reiterate your interest in the position, and await a decision. The note should be brief, but you may also want to highlight something from your conversation with the person. Remember, he or she may have met many applicants within a short period of time, so it helps to give a reminder that could jog the person's memory about your interview in particular.

Depending on the employer's needs, you may hear back within a few days, or it may take the hiring manager several weeks to make a decision. If you haven't heard anything about

Hiring managers will occasionally ask applicants to take a practical test at an interview to test their level of comfort with numbers and computers—especially with spreadsheets and other accounting software.

five business days after your first interview, you can follow up again via email or phone call. Your phone call should request to speak with the hiring manager regarding an update on your interview process. Ask if any more information is needed from you in order to assist with his or her decision.

Dealing with Rejection

Job seekers might go on many interviews before getting hired. You have to remember not to take rejection personally. It's always better that you land the job right for you, not just the first available job. If either you or the interviewer decides that you are not the best fit for the company, thank the interviewer for his or her time and humbly walk away.

Every interview, regardless of result, is a learning experience. Few are lucky enough to be offered a job right away. It takes time, patience, and a willingness to start over. Though not landing a job can be frustrating, the best thing to do is to continue sending out résumés, researching, and networking. Each interview will give you more tools and practice to apply to the next. Eventually, you will be offered a position that will be a good fit for both you and the employer.

CHAPTER FIVE

The First Day and a Lifelong Career

S tarting a new job can be exciting but also overwhelming. As a new employee, you will watch, listen, learn, and begin applying your education, training, and experience in a new setting.

Doing Paperwork

New employees usually need to take care of paperwork and other bureaucratic and administrative necessities during the first day or week on the job. Someone from the human resources department will walk you through all this paperwork, which is often known as a "new hire package." This person will probably ask you to bring in identification, such as a driver's license or Social Security card.

Many employers provide their workers with company handbooks that outline policies and procedures. That way everyone is aware of what the rules are for employee conduct regarding issues such as drug use, sexual harassment, or other inappropriate, unethical, or illegal behavior. The handbook should also explain the policies on breaks, sick days, vacation days, and other time off work.

Employees with medical insurance and other benefits, such as a pension or retirement plans, will usually receive related materials and application forms. They are also given tax forms to fill out, which determine how much in local, state, and federal income tax and Social Security tax will be deducted from their paychecks.

A new employee will be set up with his or her own station, probably including a computer and other tools needed to complete his or her tasks.

Entry-level young people on their first job can ask managers any questions about any paperwork and are encouraged to talk to parents or other experienced, working adults about these matters if they find them confusing. They need not make big decisions about benefit options hastily, but rather think about them and report back when they are ready.

The Workplace

New hires will probably be assigned their own station, cubicle, or other work area. Keeping this area neat and orderly

Because accounting employees are usually privy to sensitive information about their clients, they may be asked to sign a confidentiality agreement on their first day at work.

will make their workday run more smoothly, and it will also show supervisors and managers that the employee is organized and professional. A sloppy work area may count against workers during periodic employment reviews.

Regardless of the type of accounting they do or the industry they are part of, accountants usually work standard full-time hours. However, especially for accountants who deal with preparing tax returns, they might work overtime (and be paid accordingly, depending on the company's policy) during the busiest times of the year. Tax returns for the previous year are due to the IRS by April 15, so the months leading up to that date are often extremely hectic for all accountants. The early fall can also be busy because some companies and individuals ask the IRS for an extension, and that deadline is October 15.

The end or beginning of the fiscal year is always demanding for accountants as well. Some companies define their fiscal year differently from the calendar year. For example, the U.S. government starts its fiscal year on October 1.

Learning the Ropes

During your first few days, weeks, or months on the job, someone will probably be training you on the most important tasks and duties of your position. This might be your supervisor or a coworker who has been promoted from your job to the next level. Shadowing this person will help you learn not only how to perform your job but also about the structure and procedures of your entire department or company.

Be sure to pay attention, take notes, and ask questions whenever something is unclear. Though you may be afraid of seeming unsure of yourself, it's much better to ask at the

An untidy workspace may be a sign that an employee is disorganized and inefficient. However, be prepared to manage mountains of paperwork as part of most accounting jobs, even in the modern digital era.

beginning. If you try to figure it out on your own and make a mistake later, that could be much more costly. Whoever is training you knows that you're new and should be expecting you to have questions about how things are done around the office.

Staff Relations

Many people make friends at work, even lifelong ones. For newer members of the workforce, the workplace can feel very much like the high school or college setting they are used to. However, workers must keep things professional, separating responsibility from socializing and friendship. This can be especially important with supervisors, managers, and other superiors. Of course, this doesn't mean that you can't occasionally joke around with your colleagues or discuss things that aren't related to work. In fact, that can help break the stress or tension and help coworkers bond. However, workers should avoid inappropriate language and humor related to race and ethnicity, religion, sexual orientation or sexuality, and other controversial topics.

Having good relationships with your coworkers and supervisors is key to a positive, smooth work environment.

Many workplaces have policies discouraging or banning dating in the workplace, especially intimate relationships between managers and their subordinates, or employees. Some companies forbid employees in position of power from dating lower-level workers. Workplace rules, often documented in an employee handbook or other literature, should give new hires an idea of what they can do in case they feel harassed. Other regulations on the job forbid workers from engaging in gambling and certain financial relationships, both with coworkers and third-party contractors hired from outside the company.

In the end, such rules make the entire workplace run more smoothly. As you learn more about your coworkers' and supervisors' working styles and personalities, you will become much more comfortable.

Dealing with Clients

Just as it is important to maintain friendly but professional relationships with your coworkers, you will also need to develop a positive working relationship with your clients. Depending on what kind of accounting company you work for, clients may be individuals or businesses. A huge part of the accounting career is company and customer satisfaction. A worker in this field needs to be a "people person." Politeness, cheerfulness, and a diplomatic ability to manage client needs are almost as important as technical skill.

Any job has its fair share of deadlines, stress, and difficulty. Toward the end of the month, quarterly reporting times, and during tax season can be really stressful times. Accounting positions require you to

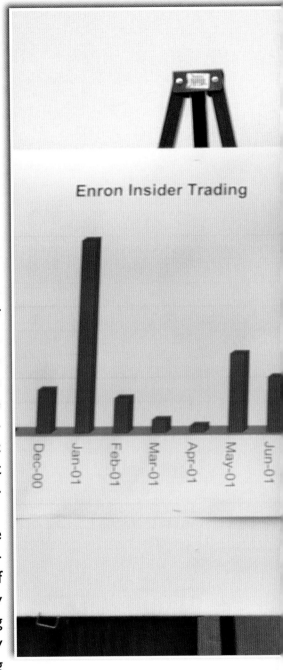

Enron Insider Trading

Dec-00 Jan-01 Feb-01 Mar-01 Apr-01 May-01 Jun-01

In 2001, the energy company Enron was found to have defrauded their shareholders of $74 billion. The fallout destroyed the company and took down its accounting firm, Arthur Andersen, formerly one of the most respected firms.

keep calm and professional in such situations. Besides being unprofessional, arguing with or insulting clients is a surefire way to get a stern lecture from a manager. Too much of it could lead to a worker getting fired.

Confidentiality

Accountants deal with a lot of sensitive personal information about both their employer and their clients. Much of this

In another accounting scandal, this one at telecommunicatons firm WorldCom in 2002, Scott Sullivan was one of several executives convicted of fraud totaling $3.8 billion.

information must be kept confidential, meaning the employee cannot reveal it to anyone outside of work. This can range from data about important business deals to individuals' Social Security numbers. Accountants might also be privy to the payroll, knowing the salaries of everyone in the company, but they would not be allowed to share that information with all of their coworkers.

There are exceptions to the rules of confidentiality: if the client authorizes the accountant to tell someone, or if the accountant is legally obligated to disclose the information in court. This might happen if a corporation is under investigation for wrongdoing and its financial records are part of the case.

New hires should make sure that they understand all the rules of confidentiality. Their company will probably have its own specific guidelines, but all accountants must also adhere to professional standards, such as the AICPA's Code of Professional Conduct. These rules may change from time to time, so accountants need to be sure they are following the most updated standards at all times.

It is crucial that you use a shredder to destroy all sensitive documents that are no longer in use, such as papers that contain clients' Social Security numbers. If any personal information was improperly disposed of, it could result in immediate termination for the violation. Protect these documents as if they are your own, and follow company policy on how to store them and dispose of them.

Further Learning

As you settle into a new job, you will feel more and more comfortable in your own role, and you'll also get to know

SPECIALIZED CERTIFICATIONS

Even beyond CPAs, there are many specialized certifications for accountants in different areas. These prove that you have become an expert in a certain topic, such as taxes, fraud, auditing, banking, or operations management. As you move up in your career, you may find that it's worth your while to pursue one of these certificates. These programs can help you distinguish yourself and become a commodity in your field.

Employers might ask an employee to earn a particular certificate within a few years of being hired. Sometimes they might pay for or reimburse someone for the cost of the program, too. Some of the certifications you might be interested in include:

- Certified Financial Planner
- Certified Management Accountant
- Certified Fraud Examiner
- Certified Internal Auditor
- Government Valuation Analyst

more about the company, its clients, and its structure. This may help you discover where you want to be as your career progresses. If you earned your associate's degree and started in an entry-level position, maybe you'll be inspired to go back to college and become a CPA. Or maybe you'll realize that you'd prefer to work for a small business rather than a large corporation. Your experiences at your first job can go a long way toward informing your future.

GLOSSARY

aggregator A website that gathers data from many other websites and displays them in one place.

aptitude A natural skill or talent for a particular task or field.

associate's degree A degree earned after a two-year program at a community college.

attestation Verification that a financial statement is accurate.

auditing The process of examining the financial accounts of an individual or institution in an official capacity.

bachelor's degree A degree earned after a four-year program at a college or university.

bookkeeping The process of recording transactions and other basic financial records.

budget An estimate of how much money will be spent and earned over a specific period of time.

bursar A person who administers the finances of a college or university.

certified public accountant (CPA) An accountant who has passed the Uniform Certified Public Accountant Examination.

confidentiality A set of rules or ethical guidelines concerning the release of private information, such as financial records.

disclose To reveal confidential information.

embezzlement Theft of money from one's employer.

fraud Deception that results in illegal financial gain.

liability A debt or other financial obligation.

money laundering The process of trying to make it seem as though money earned from criminal activity was earned through legal means.

overhead The other costs associated with a business, not including direct labor, direct materials, and direct expenses.

payroll The total wages and salaries that a company has agreed to pay all of its employees.

proprietor The owner of a business.

refund A sum of money returned to a taxpayer because the amount of taxes that were paid over the course of the year (such as those taken automatically out of a paycheck) exceeded the amount of taxes that the tax-payer owes for the year.

transaction A financial action in which money is taken out of one account and added to a different account.

FOR MORE INFORMATION

American Institute of CPAs
1211 Avenue of the Americas
New York, NY 10036-8775
(212) 596-6200
Website: http://www.aicpa.org/Pages/default.aspx
The American Institute of CPAs is the largest organization
   for people in the accounting field, with over four hun-
   dred thousand members. Its website contains helpful
   information about how to become a CPA, available
   career paths in accounting, and other career information.

The Association of Professional Accounting and Tax
   Consultants (APATC)
110 Westhunt Drive, Unit 1
Ottawa, ON K0A 1L0
Canada
(800) 429-2802
Website: http://www.apatcinc.com
APATC is a nonprofit organization for independent account-
   ing and bookkeeping firms in Canada.

Bureau of Labor Statistics
Postal Square Building
2 Massachusetts Avenue NE
Washington, DC 20212-0001
(202) 691-5200
Website: http://www.bls.gov
The Bureau of Labor Statistics provides data on employment in all different industries and fields, providing a full
   picture of the U.S. economy. It studies issues such as
   unemployment, inflation, prices, pay, and benefits. Its

website also includes student resources for exploring the economy and various careers.

Chartered Professional Accountants of Canada
277 Wellington Street West
Toronto, ON M5V 3H2
Canada
Website: http://www.cpacanada.ca
The Chartered Professional Accountants of Canada, or CPA
Canada, unites several prior professional organizations
for accountants in Canada. It provides career and profes-
sional development, as well as business and accounting
resources, for its members.

Internal Revenue Service
77 K Street NE
Washington, DC 20002
(202) 803-9000
Website: http://www.irs.gov
The IRS is the agency of the U.S. government in charge of
collecting taxes from all individuals and businesses.
Accountants need to be well versed in IRS laws and
regulations in order to report their clients' tax revenues
accurately.

National Society of Accountants
1330 Braddock Place, Suite 540
Alexandria, VA 22314
(800) 966-6679
Website: http://connect.nsacct.org/home

The National Society of Accountants is a professional organization for accountants that offers continuing education courses and webinars for people in the field.

Websites

Because of the changing nature of Internet links, Rosen Publishing has developed an online list of websites related to the subject of this book. This site is updated regularly. Please use this link to access the list:

http://www.rosenlinks.com/JOBS/account

Berger, Lauren. *All Work, No Pay: Finding an Internship, Building Your Resume, Making Connections, and Gaining Job Experience.* New York, NY: Ten Speed Press, 2012.

Boyd, Kenneth, et al. *Accounting All-in-One for Dummies.* Hoboken, NJ: John Wiley & Sons, 2014.

Boyd, Kenneth W. *CPA Exam for Dummies.* Hoboken, NJ: John Wiley & Sons, 2014.

Christen, Carol, and Richard N. Bolles. *What Color Is Your Parachute? For Teens: Discover Yourself, Design Your Future, and Plan for Your Dream Job.* 3rd ed. New York, NY: Ten Speed Press, 2015.

Citrin, James M. *The Career Playbook: Essential Advice for Today's Aspiring Young Professional.* New York, NY: Crown Business, 2015.

Consumer Dummies. Bookkeeping All-in-One for Dummies. Hoboken, NJ: John Wiley & Sons, 2015.

Covey, Sean. *The 7 Habits of Highly Effective Teens.* New York, NY: Touchstone, 2014.

Duignan, Brian, ed. *Banking and Finance* (Economics: Taking the Mystery Out of Money). New York, NY: Britannica Educational Publishing, 2013.

Giedlin, Richard. *Beat the Big 4: Real Advice to Crush Your Next Accounting Interview.* Amazon Digital Services, 2015.

Graham, Amy. *Be Smart About Your Career: College, Income, and Careers* (Be Smart About Money and Financial Literacy). Berkeley Heights, NJ: Enslow Publishers, 2014.

La Bella, Laura. *What Do I Need to Pursue a Career in Bookkeeping & Accounting?* (The Right Degree for Me). New York, NY: Rosen Publishing, 2015.

Meyer, Susan. *Careers as a Bookkeeper and Auditor* (Essential Careers). New York, NY: Rosen Publishing, 2014.

Muchnick, Justin Ross. *Teens' Guide to College and Career Planning.* 12th ed. Lawrenceville, NJ: Peterson's, 2011.

Mullis, Darrell, and Judith Orloff. *The Accounting Game: Basic Accounting Fresh from the Lemonade Stand.* Naperville, IL: Sourcebooks, 2008.

Pollak, Lindsay. *Getting from College to Career: Your Essential Guide to Succeeding in the Real World.* Rev. ed. New York, NY: Harper Business, 2012.

Sandberg, Sheryl. *Lean In for Graduates.* New York, NY: Alfred A. Knopf, 2014.

Schultze, Quentin J. *Résumé 101: A Student and Recent-Grad Guide to Crafting Résumés and Cover Letters.* New York, NY: Crown Publishing, 2012.

Yate, Martin. *Knock 'Em Dead: Secrets & Strategies for First-Time Job Seekers.* Avon, MA: Adams Media, 2013.

American Institute of CPAs. "CPA Career Paths." Retrieved March 4, 2016 (http://www.aicpa.org/Career/ CareerPaths/Pages/CareerPaths.aspx).

Association of Certified Fraud Examiners. "Forensic Accountant." Retrieved March 4, 2016 (http://www.acfe .com/career-path-forensic-accountant.aspx).

Blatch, Mary L. "AICPA's Revised Confidentiality Rule and Sec. 7216." *Journal of Accounting*, March 1, 2015. Retrieved March 3, 2016 (http://www.journalof accountancy.com/issues/2015/mar/aicpa-confidentiality-rule.html).

Brinkerhoff, John R. *101 Commonsense Rules for the Office: How to Get Along and Get Ahead.* Harrisburg, PA: Stackpole Books, 1992.

Fitzpatrick, Kathleen, and Wallace W. Kravitz. *Barron's E-Z Bookkeeping.* Hauppage, NY: Barron's Educational Series, 2010.

Half, Robert. "Guide to Certifications for Accounting, Finance and Operations Management." Accounting Web. Retrieved March 5, 2016 (http://www.accountingweb .com/sites/default/files/guide_to_certifications_robert_ half.pdf).

Ingram, David. "What Are Accounting and Auditing?" Demand Media. Retrieved March 4, 2016 (http:// smallbusiness.chron.com/auditing-accounting-11772 .html).

LinkedIn. "Tips for Teens: How to Find Your First Real Job." April 27, 2015. Retrieved March 5, 2016 (https://www .linkedin.com/pulse/tips-teens-how-find-your-first-real -job-find-jobs-candidates).

Mala, Elisa. "Teen Job Tips: 7 Things No One Tells You About Your First Job." *Huffington Post,* July 10, 2013. Retrieved March 5, 2016 (http://www.huffingtonpost.com/2013/07/10/teen-job-tips_n_3575092.html).

Marshall, Leisa. "The Sky Is the Limit—Accounting Certifications." *New Accountant.* Retrieved March 5, 2016 (http://www.newaccountantusa.com/newsfeat/ip/ip_acctcerts.html).

Monster at Work. "What HR Should Do About Manager-Subordinate Romantic Relationships." Retrieved March 5, 2016 (http://www.monster.com/about/b/hr-manager-subordinate-romantic-relationships).

Morem, Susan. *101 Tips for Graduates: A Code of Conduct for Success and Happiness in Your Professional Life.* Rev. ed. New York, NY: Checkmark Books, 2010.

Nordmeyer, Billie. "Importance of Confidentiality in Accounting." Demand Media. Retrieved March 5, 2016 (http://yourbusiness.azcentral.com/importance-confidentiality-accounting-23560.html).

Occupational Outlook Handbook. "Accountants and Auditors." Bureau of Labor Statistics, U.S. Department of Labor. Retrieved March 5, 2016 (http://www.bls.gov/ooh/business-and-financial/accountants-and-auditors.htm).

Reeves, Laurie. "The Differences Between Bookkeepers vs. Accountants vs. CPAs." Demand Media. Retrieved March 2, 2016 (http://work.chron.com/differences-between-bookkeepers-vs-accountants-vs-cpas-4173.html).

Tracy, John A. *Accounting for Dummies.* 5th ed. Hoboken, NJ: John Wiley & Sons, 2013.

INDEX

A

accounting
   certificates in, 28–30, 68
   confidentiality in, 66–67
   degrees in, 31
   difference between bookkeeping
      and, 13–14
   double-entry, 11
   education for, 5, 14, 15, 20–33, 68
   functions of, 4–5, 7–8, 15–17
   jobs, 5, 8–13
   types of, 15
American Institute of Certified
      Public Accountants (AICPA),
      18, 67

B

bookkeeping, 13–14, 21, 28, 31
   education for, 14

C

certified public accountants, 5, 6, 7,
      14, 27, 31–33, 42, 68
   education for, 31–33
   qualifications of, 17–18, 32
   rules for, 18
community college, 28
company accountant, 8–9
cover letters, 39

D

double-entry accounting, 11

E

employment websites, 39–41

F

financial aid, 25–30
   types of, 29
Free Application for Federal
      Student Aid (FAFSA), 29

G

General Educational Development
      (GED), 14
grants, 29
guidance counselor, 20–21, 26

H

high school, 20–21
   college courses in, 22–25

I

Internal Revenue Service (IRS), 8,
      59

About the Author

Amy Beattie is a writer from New Hampshire. A former Outward Bound instructor, she has counseled many teens who are applying to college and their first jobs.

Photo Credits

Cover, p. 1, (figure) Neustockimages/E+/Getty Images; cover, p. 1 (background), interior pages, back cover Vasco/E+/Getty Images; p. 6 Steve Weinrebe/Photographer's Choice/Getty Images; p. 9 i love images/Cultura/Getty Images; pp. 10, 66 Bloomberg/Getty Images; pp. 12-13 Westend61/Getty Images; pp. 16-17 Justin Sullivan/Getty Images; pp. 22-23 Blend Images-Hill Street Studios/Brand X Pictures/Getty Images; pp. 24-25 Joe Amon/The Denver Post/Getty Images; p. 27 Peter Glass/Photolibrary/Getty Images; p. 30 © Tribune Content Agency LLC/Alamy Stock Photo; p. 32 Tim Boyle/Getty Images; p. 35 PeopleImages/E+/Getty Images; p. 37 Spencer Platt/Getty Images; p. 41 © NetPics/Alamy Stock Photo; pp. 42-43 Hans Neleman/The Image Bank/Getty Images; p. 47 Hero Images/Getty Images; pp. 50-51 CaiaImage/Getty Images; p. 52 Courtney Keating/E+/Getty Images; p. 54 Anthony Johnson/The Image Bank/Getty Images; p. 57 John Lamb/Photographer's Choice/Getty Images; p. 58 © juan moyano/Alamy Stock Photo; pp. 60-61 Roberto Machado Noa/LightRocket/Getty Images; pp. 62-63 skynesher/E+/Getty Images; pp. 64-65 Douglas Graham/CQ-Roll Call Group/Getty Images

Designer: Nicole Russo; Editor: Philip Wolny;
Photo Researcher: Philip Wolny